Hood Love 3:

Take Heed To The Warnings

R4Presents.tictail.com

ISBN-13: 978-1986415248
ISBN-10: 1986415244
Copyright©2018 by Danielle Bigsby/Royal 4 Publishing Presents

Special discounts are available on quantity purchases by corporations, associations, and others as determined by Royal 4 Publishing Presents. Orders may also be shipped to penal and correctional facilities.

Merchandise available at:
R4Presents.tictail.com

Hood Love 3:

Take Heed to The Warnings

By:

Danielle Bigsby

<u>Acknowledgements</u>

I first want to thank God for blessing me with the talent and ability of expressing myself through words. I also want to thank Him for implanting the vision of conveying a message through my gift that He has blessed me with. Without Him, I wouldn't exist and none of this would be possible.

I want to thank my children: Eniyah, Te'Ontez, Danterryia, and Da'Nae; for always pushing and motivating me to constantly become better and grow daily.

I also would like to thank my entire support team for not allowing me to give up when things looked rough. I love and thank each of you from the bottom of my heart.

I want to send special hugs and love to each family that has allowed me the chance to share their loved one's story with the world. I am forever grateful to you for entrusting me to enlighten the world on the issue of gun violence through your loved one's tragic story. I love each of you and am here for you in any way that I can be.

Lastly, to my Royalties and Rawyalties, I thank you for taking the time to read my books and leave feedback. I will never take you for granted. You are my inspiration and motivation to continue doing what I love to do. I truly thank you as well as appreciate you royally.

<u>Dedication</u>

◆This one is dedicated to all victims of gun violence and the families who've had to suffer through the loss of a loved one due to gun violence.

◆This book is for the friends left behind to cherish the memories.

◆This book is for the children who must now grow up without parents because guns took them away.

◆And finally, this book is for the youth who feel pressured to become a part of the streets because they feel no one understands them.

I only have one request of you...

◆Put down the guns and just LIVE!!! Your life is way too valuable and the streets will only rob you of it.

<u>Table of Contents</u>

Hear My Plea

A single tear escapes from eyes,

As I stare off in space...

I hate this time of year,

My mind lives in constant fear;

Wondering if another round of bullets will take another one of

my children away from me.

I can't wrap gifts,

Or see their smiling faces;

I can't force my heart be at ease,

For that fateful day lives on repeat in my mind,

And no matter how hard I try,

I can't stop crying.

I'd give my life,

To see my child once again laughing and playing,

But that'll never be,

So my heart remains forever lodged in pure agony.

Nothing I do,

Can ever bring my baby back,

Danielle Bigsby

And that's what hurts the most;

But I'll keep living,

For it's my only option,

While I hold on to the hope and notion that my child's case will

one day save someone's life.

One day,

Someone'll hear the message in their death;

They'll realize bullets have no eyes,

They'll see that once you pull the trigger,

You can't take it back.

My child's story will hopefully inspire them to put down the

guns,

And just live;

Because we truly only get one life to live.

Gun violence usually ends in one of two ways,

A jail cell,

Or a grave.

Someone's loved ones must bury them,

While someone else's child ends up locked up;

That's a double loss any way you look at it.

So again, I say,

Put down the guns,

And just live!

Take heed to the messages in the stories of those lives lost

before you,

Warning comes before destruction;

And I'd hate to see you walking in those same shoes,

When you don't have to.

Chapter 1: The Reality of It All

Ain't no loyalty in the streets. You're nothing more than an expendable piece on the street's chess board. The streets are easy to get into, but hard to get out of. Don't be another casualty. Make your life count for something.

Danielle Bigsby

<u>Who Do You Trust</u>

The streets taught me so much,

Both in life,

And in death.

They showed me how to get a quick dollar,

And then stunt on the block;

Yet they also kept me up a many of nights,

With my gun cocked.

They showed me love,

When I was at the top of my game doing all the wrong things;

Yet regarded me as a nobody the moment I decided to change

my life for the better.

Many of my "homies" ate at my table,

Both literally and figuratively,

Then conspired with my enemies to take everything from me.

I valued friendship,

But learned the hard way,

That everybody with you ain't for you.

How could the same one I laughed with,

Help bring about my demise?

How could some of the very ones I loved,

Be the same ones my family now despises?

I spent my most valuable years loving a life that loves no one,

And just when I started to get it right,

I died.

It's too late for me,

But you can still change,

I just hope and pray you will,

Before it's too late.

Dedicated to the loving memory of Georgio Gray

The Only Way

So much has been said,

About how I died,

Yet most criticized me,

When I was alive.

No one cared about my wellbeing,

As long as I did what they wanted me to;

Yet now that I'm gone,

They're all singing my praises.

I could care less,

About the nice things said at my funeral once I was dead,

Because none of those sentiments were shared,

When I really needed to hear them.

You see,

Hearing the good could have saved the streets from claiming

me.

If only I had been encouraged to be all I could be,

I would have had a significantly lower chance of someone killing

me.

Danielle Bigsby

Perhaps if someone had shown me something different,

I wouldn't have been attracted to the glitz and glamour of the

streets,

And a victim of gun violence,

I wouldn't be.

But they didn't,

So I got it how I lived;

Robbing,

Stealing,

Even killing,

Just to survive;

But in the end,

None of that kept me alive.

So I said all that to say this,

Take back our youth,

Do it today;

For that is the only way to stop this epidemic;

The only way,

For lives to truly be saved.

**Dedicated to the memories of every young life lost to gun
violence**

<u>Restricted by Silence</u>

Lots of hearsay,

But when the detectives come around,

No one has anything to say.

Nearly eight years,

And yall still talking about snitching,

But when the shoe's on the other foot,

You want everybody to sing like canaries.

You have the keys to solve my case,

With what you heard and saw,

But you won't give it up,

Because it goes against the code.

That's some real sad shit there,

Especially when you claimed to have loved me;

You can sit back and watch my mother cry,

Without an ounce of remorse,

But you say you have a heart.

You even cry crocodile tears on demand,

For both my birthday and death anniversary,

But what about all the other days in between?

Do you even miss me?

Truth be told,

You don't even know my birthday,

Unless one of my family members make a post on Facebook;

And the only reason my death anniversary is celebrated or

thought of,

Is when the homie Twan, connects it to his birthday celebration

and turn up.

I've been reduced to nothing more than a conversation piece,

And judging by the unsolved status of my case,

Many are talking,

Just not to the detective's face;

Leaving my family to hope and pray,

That someone gains a conscious,

Leading them to finally speak up someday.

Dedicated in honor of the loving memory of Ronquez Bigsby

Make It Right

You'll know when it's your time to go,

If you're in tune with God,

You'll hear that soft whisper,

As unsettling feelings sweep over your body,

Urging you to tell those that you love,

"I love you",

Just one more time.

A nagging need to get your life in order,

Pulls at you,

With the intent of allowing your soul,

To rest at ease.

While you know that you gotta go,

Simply because we all must die,

You don't know exactly when, how, or why?

Still you push on,

Striving to make amends for past mistakes and wrongdoings,

Trying your damnedest,

To make everything right.

Praying you go peacefully,

Asking God to remove all fear;

Crying secretly,

So no one sees your tears.

Aiming to please God,

By completing His mission in your final days,

Seeking wise counsel from your pastor,

Preparing to depart from this corrupt world.

Preparations made,

You've prayed your final prayer,

Now you're all set;

But no man truly knows the day or hour,

And God never revealed to you,

The fact that your life would be stolen,

Due to the reckless actions of a silly coward.

He couldn't show you,

The horrific scene you'd have to endure,

Because He knew you'd back out;

According to him however,

You'd suffered enough.

And as contradicting as it sounds,

That coward's actions allowed you to be free,

From any more pain,

Hurt,

Or agony;

Your soul no longer has a care in the world,

No more tears,

No more sadness,

No more worries,

No more stress;

Just eternal rest…

✟✟✟

I asked God to look after my family,

And He assured me that I don't have to worry,

Because He watches over them in both their good and their

bad;

That stands as the proof that He heard my prayers before I left

Earth.

If I had to ask one thing of my family,

It would be,

Make amends with each other,

And get it right;

If for nobody else,

Please do it for me.

Dedicated to the loving memory of Tyrone Reece

Danielle Bigsby

Make It Count

Well known,

Liked by everyone;

Yet my life still ended at the hands of a gun.

A protector,

A true friend,

Known as the sweet and gentle giant;

A blessing to many,

A man sorely missed,

No matter what went on in my life,

I didn't deserve this.

All the love I gave out,

Didn't stop someone from taking my life,

And that alone speaks volumes.

It doesn't matter if my actions were good, bad, or indifferent,

No one has the right to rob another person of their life.

See the message in my story,

Because it's prevalent,

No one knows when death will come a knocking,

So make the best of your life,

While you still can;

Because once you're six feet under,

It's all over.

There'll be no chance to go back,

And fix what you didn't get right.

So again I say,

Make the best of your life.

Dedicated to the loving memory of Keith Battle

Loyal to Death

My hands were nothing to play with,

But that means nothing in today's society;

People scared,

They don't fight fair anymore,

Leading them to bring guns to a fist fight.

I just wanted my respect,

And yes,

I was willing to fight for mine,

Who knew I wouldn't come out alive.

I had plans for a big birthday party,

That was just a few weeks away,

And truth be told,

It wasn't my fight anyway.

Actually,

I was just there to watch,

And make sure nobody ganged my girl,

But I never made it out the car.

Bullets tore into my side of the car,

Slowly stripping away my life,

And all I could do,

Was pray that I made it out alright.

It looked hopeful when I was transported to Vanderbilt hospital,

But fate wouldn't prevail in my favor,

My young fifteen-year-old life was now over.

I died because of someone else's beef,

The shit didn't even have anything to do with me;

So much for loyalty,

Because at the end of the day,

It couldn't save me.

Dedicated to the loving memory of RowNeshia Overton

A Thing of The Past

Forgotten without a trace,

No longer remembered,

Or even remotely celebrated,

By anyone outside those that were closest to me.

No follow up news stories,

No new leads,

Nor any additional information;

I've been reduced to nothing more than a case file on some

disinterested officer's messy desk.

My mom still cries herself to sleep every night,

Wondering why;

Why did they have to take away her son?

Why did it even have to happen at all?

Then comes the thoughts of what;

What could she have done differently to save my life?

What if she'd just gotten there sooner?

And then more thoughts of why it even happened in the first

place;

What was the purpose in killing her baby?

What did they stand to achieve?

Where were my friends when all this happened?

Why didn't they help me?

Could my friends have been involved?

Why was no one talking?

Why was no one telling what they saw?

Torturous thoughts swim through her head on a nightly basis,

And she can't seem to find any relief from the grief,

Because she'll never be able to get any rest,

Until she at least knows why they did this to me.

The more time that passes by,

The less hope she has,

That she will one day get answers,

To those silent prayers for justice,

That lie written across her heart.

Stuck in time,

As she constantly relives that moment she lost me,

Over and over again.

I pray,

That someone has a heart,

And finally speaks up,

Because my mom's poor heart has suffered enough.

Dedicated to the loving memory of Antoine Meeks

<u>Who Knew</u>

Visiting my girl,

Chilling,

Having a good time;

Then my phone rings,

Forcing me to head outside;

To the basketball court for a split second,

But much to my surprise,

Those moments became the last ones of my life.

I never thought my life would really end,

Especially so soon;

I had children that I wanted to make it back to.

So much to live for,

So much I wanted to accomplish,

So many unanswered questions,

And still no trace of my killer.

Three years later,

And I'm officially a cold case,

Just another gun violence statistic,

With a forgotten face.

In the blink of an eye,

My life was over;

So badly do I wish,

I had the chance to do it all over;

But I can't,

And my family along with other loved ones,

must live with that fact.

If asked what I would say to those alive,

It would be,

Live your life,

Happy and free;

Think before you act,

Because once you take a life,

You can't give it back;

No matter how many times you say that you're sorry,

It won't do much to ease the fact,

That you took away someone's loved one,

And there's no way to bring them back.

Dedicated to the loving memory of John Sykes

In Our Shoes

No parent wants to bury their child,

That's not the way it should be,

Simply because,

I shouldn't outlive my child.

No child should witness the gruesome death of their parent

either,

Especially at the hands of a gun,

Forever haunted by the memories,

That nothing they could've done would or could have saved

you;

For fear held them captive,

Simply because they were just too young.

No community should be robbed of such innocent lives,

Forced to watch the next generation quickly vanishing,

Right before their eyes.

No school should be stripped of its future leaders,

Watching so much potential die before it gets the chance to

fully flourish.

No individual should live in fear,

Danielle Bigsby

Of the very ones charged with their protection,

Wondering if they'll make it back home to their families,

Every night.

Our shoes,

Aren't ones I'd wish on my worst enemy,

The void left behind,

My empty, broken heart;

No, I wouldn't wish that on anyone.

I beg, plead, and pray;

That our youth opens their eyes,

To see the devastation caused by this unrelenting epidemic,

Before their family winds standing in our shoes.

It's our hope,

That the stories of our loved ones,

Serve as a warning before destruction,

Shielding them from this tragic path;

For if at least one life is saved or changed,

The deaths of our loved ones won't have been in vain.

Hear the message in their deaths,

Is all we ask,

At the end of the day.

[38]

Put down the guns,

Enjoy your lives,

And thank God for the opportunity to see another day!

Dedicated to any and everyone that has lost a loved one due

to gun violence

<u>No Loyalty</u>

They'll act a fool at your funeral,

Fall over your casket crying,

Damn near collapse when they put you in the ground,

Post memories all over their social media;

Then scream free your killer.

Truth be told,

Most of them knew your killer from the start,

But refuse to help your family get justice,

Because they'll be viewed as a snitch,

Not realizing,

In the eyes of real street cats,

They're already coming across as a scared little bitch.

Ain't no loyalty in the streets,

Because the streets don't love nobody;

So be careful of the ones you choose to befriend,

For once your body is cold in the ground,

Most will quickly forget you even existed...

Chapter 2: See It, Hear It, Feel It

Some things serve as a warning before destruction and that's exactly what these victims and their stories seek to do. They aim to warn you of what's to come if you decide to pull the trigger of a gun. Take heed to their warnings so that you don't end up like they did. Don't be a casualty; be a story of triumph instead.

Danielle Bigsby

It Ain't Right

It ain't right...

My life might not have been lived the way they thought it
should have been,
That however,
Gave them no right to take it.

Where I'm from,
You don't stop when you see the police,
You wait until you're in a place where someone can see you;
Because if you do stop,
You're sure to wind up being a casualty;
And sadly,
That's what happened to me.

I was surrounded by hopelessness daily,
Yet my family gave me a reason to be hopeful;
And my spirit is pained that they must live on without me.

We're taught to trust the red, white, and blue to protect us,
Yet they're the very ones who took away my precious life.

Statistics,

Criminal records,

My neighborhood,

And my skin,

Were the ultimate deciding factors for me to live or die;

Yet if they knew these things,

They should have understood my apprehension and fear.

Our lives haven't mattered in history,

And in that neighborhood,

They still don't;

Every time a policeman rolls through,

Panic is heightened.

Look around the country,

And you will see,

Why my fight or flight system kicked in.

An unfortunate tragedy is what they called it,

Murder is what I say;

And as usual,

White cop,

Black male victim,

Not guilty at the end of the day.

My life mattered,

And it still does!

While nothing will bring me back,

Taking a stance adds value to my memory.

Don't take the news for face value,

Research my case for yourself,

Ask my loved ones about me,

Then you will see,

Why my mother, Sheila Clemmons-Lee, and the rest of my loved

ones fight daily,

To ensure that Officer Lippert is held accountable for what he

did to me.

Dedicated to the loving memory of Jocques Clemmons

Danielle Bigsby

<u>My Eyes Have Seen</u>

The haunting nightmares,

Are forever ingrained in my head,

Of that fateful, unfortunate day,

They took my daddy away.

I was young,

But that doesn't mean I don't know what happened;

You see,

Everywhere my daddy went,

He took me.

And on that day,

I stood between the two people who loved me the most,

Feeling like the most blessed child alive;

But in a matter of seconds,

It all changed.

Daddy was talking,

Then they were arguing,

As mommy held me at her side,

Awaiting daddy's return;

But that would never be.

Daddy fell,

Mommy screamed,

And I cried;

As we witnessed the man I loved the most,

Losing his life.

There I stood,

At the tender age of three,

Looking at the lost soul of the man who created me.

Everything happened so fast,

And I didn't really understand,

That daddy was never coming back.

He'll never be able to see me play sports,

Or walk across the stage;

Nor will I ever again see that big smile on his face,

From me making him proud.

I'm his twin,

And when I look in the mirror,

His reflection stares back at me.

I know he lives on,

Because of me,

And for that reason,

He'll never forgotten.

The pictures and memories,

Are all I have left of him,

And it hurts;

Because no one deserves to witness the dreaded image of their

father,

Dying violently right before their little innocent eyes.

So when you look at me,

See the devastation created from an unnecessary tragedy;

And know that when you pull that trigger,

You're changing someone's child,

For the rest of their life.

Dedicated to the loving memory of Ronnie Foxx in honor of his

one and only son RJ

Danielle Bigsby

Just Live

The way I lived my life,

Nor which gender I chose to identify with,

Matters;

My live held value,

And no one had the right to strip that precious gift away from

me.

Certain things may be considered taboo,

But taking a life for fear of judgement,

Is never the solution.

My blood bled red,

Just like everyone else;

And despite what some may have thought,

Nothing was wrong with me!

Yet the hostility towards those who choose to live life on their

own terms such as me,

Is what led to the final moments of my life.

Awareness,

Communication,

Acceptance,

[53]

And understanding,

Could have all saved my life,

Because at the end of the day,

The events that led up to my death,

Just weren't right.

They talked about Jesus,

And they're sure to talk about you too;

No gun can stop that.

So live your life,

Put down these guns,

And remember,

They're going to talk about you no matter what you do!

Dedicated to the loving memory of Gilbert "Gizzy" Fowler

The Void

The oldest,

The goofy one,

The one with the biggest heart;

The one they called Lucky.

The first one to gain a piece of my heart;

My strength,

When I no longer felt strong;

The motivation pushing me forward,

When I felt I could no longer go on;

And now you're gone.

Almost three years since I was forced to depart from you,

Each day it gets harder and harder to accept,

Rivers of emotion,

Cascade down my face;

As I realize the damage left behind.

Sometimes it's anger,

Because they robbed your son of a father;

Or maybe it's because your siblings were robbed of their role

model.

Sometimes it's tears of sadness,

Because there's a void in my heart,

That'll never be filled;

No matter what I do.

Most times,

It's the gut wrenching pain,

Of having to bury my child;

That's been building day after day,

Since that painfully numbing day,

That cowards with guns took my first born away.

A day I'll never forget,

A moment in time I'll always regret;

Even though there's nothing I could've done,

I will forever regret,

Not being there to protect my son.

I try my best to cope,

But looking at my grandson,

Causes sobs to remain lodged in my throat.

I hate that he's forced to grow up without his father,

And I pray every day,

That his father's spirit surrounds him in every way.

I'm grateful and blessed,

That my son was able to leave a legacy behind,

But this didn't have to be.

So I beg of you,

Put down the guns and just live,

So no other mother,

Has to ever feel like me.

Dedicated to the loving memory of Dejuan Lytle in honor of his mother Broderica Hamlett

<u>Fleeting Seconds</u>

Safety,

That was the only thing on my mind.

I needed to get to my loved ones,

So they could help me;

I couldn't stop running if I'd wanted to,

Yet my blood moved faster than my feet,

Pushing my body to the limits.

If I could only make it,

Just a little bit further;

Thoughts racing,

Scared out of my mind,

But I must keep going,

Because I ain't ready to die.

Everything's going faint,

My body's getting weak,

I'm trying so hard,

But I just can't seem to move my feet.

Darkness is coming,

My body's growing heavy,

"Control your breathing",

My mind says,

"Slow and steady";

But my body doesn't seem to comprehend,

And the surrender of life slowly begins.

This is it,

I can't go on;

My life flashes before my eyes,

And I finally realize,

That I won't be making it home.

This is it,

The final seconds of my life;

No time to tell my mother that I love her,

No time left to right my wrongs,

No time to say my goodbyes,

No time left to enjoy my life,

As my soul has been called home.

My life is now another tragic death,

Just another tale of gun violence,

In Nashville's streets,

Leaving my family,

To live on without me.

Dedicated to the loving memory of Rogerick Jenkins

Danielle Bigsby

In Plain Sight

For years I wondered who did this to you,

I even wondered if I'd ever get answers in my lifetime.

Many nights I cried myself to sleep,

Wondering if I'd stared your killer in the face;

Did I see them daily?

Were they hidden in plain sight?

Or did they remain in the shadows,

For fear of getting caught?

Did I know them personally?

Was there more than one killer?

And if there were,

What made them take my mom away?

Fate however intervened,

Revealing my mom's killer before I left this earth,

And what saddens me the most,

Is that after destroying the lives of my family,

Their conscious never kicked in.

Taking away someone's mom wasn't enough,

To end their life of crime,

In fact,

My mom's death was just one of the many criminal acts,

Committed by her killers.

As it turns out,

Some of my own family knew the men that did it,

Which only resulted in more questions.

No matter how many days of trial I sit through;

No matter how many days in jail they're going to have to serve;

No matter how many apologies they give;

It'll never be enough!

No punishment is fitting or sufficient enough when it comes to

my mother's life!

They took her away,

On the day of one of the most precious celebrations of my life,

The day her smile beamed with pride,

The day joyous sparks filled her eyes,

The day she celebrated her pride and joy's walk across the

stage,

The day that started out so beautiful,

Now brings me constant nightmares.

They watched my agonizing journey,

As I tirelessly searched for her killer;

They witnessed the heartbreaking sorrow,

Each time I told our story to reporters, newspapers, gun

violence summits, youth conferences, and unsolved murder

panelists;

They even viewed the countless gun violence marches through

the neighborhood,

In the flesh,

As they stood undetected in plain sight.

ঙ৯৯

I thank God for science,

You see,

Because of it,

My mother's killers no longer possess the right,

To stand in my eyesight;

Except in the presence of a jury,

As they await their fate.

It took roughly ten years,

To get a sliver of justice,

And while it'll never bring my mother back,

I'm at least comforted by the fact,

That life as those bastards once knew it,

Is over!

Dedicated to the loving memory of Cheryl Phillips in honor of

her daughter Jacketa Bell

The Essence of Me

Granny's baby,

That's what I was;

And even after reuniting in the afterlife,

My heart's still uneasy;

Simply because,

The world never got the true essence of me.

I never got the opportunity to leave behind a little me,

Whose sole purpose would've been shining light on my legacy.

I was robbed of the chance,

To create a child,

The chance to raise someone to be better than me;

They cheated a child of a life filled with love, lessons, and

blessings;

And I, of the chance to show the world that I was raised right.

I may have done my dirt,

But that didn't reveal who I truly was;

The essence of my heart,

Was nothing but love.

I saw the good in everyone,

And that ultimately wound up being my biggest flaw.

My big heart trusted way too much,

And even against very good advice,

I never imagined people that I referred to as friends,

Being the ones to end my life.

The pain I felt as I lay there dying,

Could never compare to the pain and heartache that my family

felt,

When they found out they'd lost me for good.

A close knit,

Tight,

United family we were;

My heart pains,

When they must gather for family gatherings without me,

For they were the only ones to know the man,

That I aspired to be.

If I could say anything,

It would be,

Live your life to the fullest,

While setting goals for yourself;

[68]

Stay focused,

And away from the streets,

Take heed to advice given,

And please, please, please trust your instincts;

So you won't end up like me.

Dedicated to the loving memory of Anton Irvin

Danielle Bigsby

[70]

<u>Letter from The Grave</u>

I defended you,

When others told me not to;

Who knew you'd grow balls,

And kill me.

I had you around my family,

Including my kids;

And even though we went through times of friction,

I never imagined it would end up like this.

You knew my life inside and out;

You knew how I got down;

And as I look back on it now,

I realize that's the reasoning behind your actions.

You feared my clap back,

And you knew under the right circumstances,

I'd get you,

Before I let you get me.

You knew you had to capitalize,

Because if you didn't,

My face would haunt you,

Until I ultimately ended your life.

Scared people do crazy things,

And you feared me with everything in you,

Which forced you to do what you felt you had to do.

Cowardly,

Fear is also what led to your capture;

You perpetuated the image of a hard core gangsta,

As you walked the streets with a rifle in your hands,

Yet you surrendered to them jump out boys without incident.

You killed me,

Yet you were too scared to die;

Not only that,

You feared the consequences coming from my family,

So you let the police take you to jail instead.

If that ain't a bitch move,

I don't know what is.

If you gone be man enough to pull the trigger,

Be man enough to deal with the consequences that come with

it.

I ain't saying shooting up the block is cool,

But when it comes to defending yourself or the lives of the ones

you love,

You gotta do what you gotta do.

I didn't want this life,

It chose me;

Forcing my dream of being a basketball star,

To be put on hold,

As I provided for my seeds.

The clock on my life expired prematurely however,

Never allowing me the chance,

To pick back up my dreams,

All because my reputation of being one not to be played with,

Preceded me.

No time to get it right now;

I just hope my brothers, sisters, nieces and nephews all strive to

achieve their dreams,

And let nothing get in their way;

For beating the odds is all that matters,

At the end of the day.

It is my hope that my children become a success story as well,

And that they know that I'm watching them from up above,

All the while sending them and their mothers my love.

And to the youth I say,

Just live while you still have the chance;

These streets usually end in one of two ways,

A jail cell,

Or a grave;

Avoid this path at all costs,

As you can see,

I didn't make it out;

So please put down the guns,

And just live;

So you can at least go on,

To make your mothers proud.

Dedicated to the loving memory of Antonio Kelly

<u>My Dear Mother</u>

A young man,

Barely out of high school,

Full of life,

With dreams and things that I aspired to be;

But a bullet delivered an unfortunate fate,

On October 23, 2015;

Such a sad and tragic day it was.

My mom's only child,

Her source of pride and joy,

Her movie watching buddy,

The creator of some of her biggest headaches;

And I'm saddened by the void my death left behind.

Nothing can ever bring me back,

Meaning,

No one will ever be able to truly heal her broken heart;

And that hurts.

Although I couldn't have stopped this tragedy,

The loss of me,

Has solely been responsible for her greatest heartache and pain.

[75]

If I could change the events of that day,

I would in a heartbeat;

I'd give anything,

To see her smile wholeheartedly again.

My mother was more than a mother,

She was my best friend,

And I just want to see her happy again.

I know having me alive,

Would give her the greatest joy;

But since that's not an option,

I can help orchestrate quite a few things from up above.

Even in heaven,

I'm still screening men;

He better come correct,

If it's her heart that he's trying to win.

And her career will be filled with success,

Because when it comes to accomplishing goals,

My mom's the best!

Moms are a son's first example of what a woman should be,

And even though my years of life were cut short,

I must thank God for sharing the best woman on Earth with me!

If I had to leave a thought with you,

It would be,

Cherish the woman that gave you life;

Make her proud;

Keep a smile on her face;

Because no one can ever take your mother's place.

I love you Mom!

Dedicated to Kendra Reeves in loving memory of Jory Sweatt

Know Your Worth

Eye candy to the ladies,

Both intelligent and fine;

And with attributes like that

I was bound to create a few haters.

I didn't splurge,

Or stunt,

Or try to show out;

Just being me,

And doing my own thing,

Is all I was about.

Still I was hated,

For reasons, I was never quite able to understand.

They desired what I had;

They truly wanted to be in my shoes;

So bad,

That they even conspired and plotted to take my position.

What started out as a robbery,

End up stealing my life.

Envy and jealousy,

Were the root causes of my demise,

But it didn't have to be that way.

◆ ◆ ◆ ◆ ◆

A lesson is to be learned from my death,

A lesson of self-reflection;

Learn to love you,

And all the things it takes to make you who you are;

Then they'll be no room for jealousy and envy in your heart,

Simply because,

You'll be too blinded by the shine of your own star.

Dedicated to the loving memory of Isaac Hutcherson

<u>The Choice Is Yours</u>

You are the controller of your destiny,

How far you go in life depends on the choices you make;

You and only you,

Possess the power needed to make your life great.

Circumstances may have been unfortunate,

And life may have dealt you a bad hand,

But perception however,

Is the key.

Is the glass half empty?

Or is it half full?

Will it make you?

Or will you let it break you?

Will you learn from other's mistakes?

Or are you destined to repeat them?

Are you a leader?

Or are you just another follower?

Are you going to be a success story?

Or will you be labeled as nothing more than a failure?

Will you be another sad and unfortunate tragedy?

Or will you be the one to triumph?

Will you make it out?

It's all up to you,
Be more than they said you would;
Go further than they said you could;
Don't become a statistic;

Take the hand you were dealt,
And make the best of it!

Dedicated to every youth fighting to make it out

Chapter 3: The Faces of Gun Violence

We are what gun violence looks like. We are the tragic casualties of this epidemic. See our faces and feel our family's pain. Think of the consequences to come before you pull that trigger.

#SayOurNames

#NeverForget

#PutDownTheGuns

#JustLIVE

I am the face of gun violence…

I am Ronquez "Quez" Bigsby

Birthdate: October 16, 1995

Death Date: August 11, 2010

Age at time of death: 14

Age he would be in 2018: 23

Your Memory Lives On Ronquez

#SayMyName   #NeverForget

I am the face of gun violence...

I am Cheryl Phillips

Birthdate: April 28, 1968

Death Date: May 23, 2006

Age at time of death: 38

Age she would be in 2018: 50

Children Left To Cherish Her Memory: 1 (Jacketa Bell)

Your Memory Lives On Cheryl

#SayMyName #NeverForget

I am the face of gun violence...

I am Antonio "Tony" Kelly

Birthdate: March 24, 1991

Death Date: February 28, 2011

Age at time of death: 19

Age he would be in 2018: 27

Children Left To Cherish His Memory: 3 (Antanesha Tibbs;

La'Shonti Tibbs; Dashawn Henderson)

Your Memory Lives On Antonio

#SayMyName   #NeverForget

I am the face of gun violence...

I am Tyrone Reece

Birthdate: May 9, 1983

Death Date: June 21, 2013

Age at time of death: 30

Age he would be in 2018: 35

Children Left To Cherish His Memory: 5

Your Memory Lives On Tyrone

#SayMyName   #NeverForget

I am the face of gun violence...

I am Anton "Juve" Irvin

Birthdate: March 27, 1985

Death Date: March 28, 2008

Age at time of death: 23

Age he would be in 2018: 33

Your Memory Lives On Anton

#SayMyName   #NeverForget

I am the face of gun violence...

I am Lamar "Money Mar" Hughes

Birthdate: December 6, 1993

Death Date: September 5, 2010

Age at time of death: 16

Age he would be in 2018: 25

Your Memory Lives On Lamar

#SayMyName   #NeverForget

I am the face of gun violence...

I am Keith "Big Ke" Battle

Birthdate: December 9, 1981

Death Date: June 16, 2015

Age at time of death: 33

Age he would be in 2018: 37

Your Memory Lives On Keith

#SayMyName   #NeverForget

I am the face of gun violence...

I am Jory Sweatt

Birthdate: December 3, 1995

Death Date: October 22, 2015

Age at time of death: 19

Age he would be in 2018: 23

Your Memory Lives On Jory

#SayMyName   #NeverForget

I am the face of gun violence...

I am RowNeshia Overton

Birthdate: June 16, 1999

Death Date: May 26, 2015

Age at time of death: 15

Age she would be in 2018: 19

Your Memory Lives On RowNeshia

#SayMyName   #NeverForget

I am the face of gun violence...

I am Isaac "I Ball" Hutcherson

Birthdate: January 18, 1977

Death Date: June 29, 2005

Age at time of death: 28

Age he would be in 2018: 41

Your Memory Lives On Isaac

#SayMyName   #NeverForget

I am the face of gun violence...

I am Antione Meeks

Birthdate: October 20, 1984

Death Date: December 1, 2003

Age at time of death: 19

Age he would be in 2018: 32

Children Left To Cherish His Memory: 1

Your Memory Lives On Antione

#SayMyName   #NeverForget

I am the face of gun violence...

I am John "Black" Sykes

Birthdate: December 19, 1981

Death Date: April 29, 2015

Age at time of death: 33

Age he would be in 2018: 37

Children Left Behind To Cherish His Memory: 7

Your Memory Lives On John

#SayMyName   #NeverForget

I am the face of gun violence...

I am Jocques Clemmons

Birthdate: March 30, 1985

Death Date: February 10, 2017

Age at time of death: 31

Age he would be in 2018: 33

Children Left To Cherish His Memory: 2(Biological) 6 (Step)

Your Memory Lives On Jocques

#SayMyName   #NeverForget

I am the face of gun violence...

I am Dejuan "Lucky" Lytle

Birthdate: December 10, 1998

Death Date: July 14, 2015

Age at time of death: 16

Age he would be in 2018: 19

Children Left To Cherish His Memory: 1 (De'Mario)

Your Memory Lives On Dejuan

#SayMyName   #NeverForget

I am the face of gun violence...

I am Ronnie Foxx

Birthdate: October 4, 1996

Death Date: May 9, 2016

Age at time of death: 20

Age he would be in 2018: 22

Children Left Behind To Cherish His Memory: 1 (Ronnie Foxx, Jr.)

Your Memory Lives On Ronnie

#SayMyName   #NeverForget   #SOLOMONDAYS

I am the face of gun violence...

I am Gilbert "Gizzy" Fowler

Birthdate: August 28,1990

Death Date: November 12, 2014

Age at time of death: 24

Age he would be in 2018: 28

Your Memory Lives On Gilbert

#SayMyName   #NeverForget

I am the face of gun violence…

I am Rogerick "RaRa" Jenkins

Birthdate: February 3, 1992

Death Date: April 25, 2015

Age at time of death: 23

Age he would be in 2018: 26

Your Memory Lives On Rogerick

#SayMyName   #NeverForget

I am the face of gun violence...

I am Georgio Gray

Birthdate: June 11, 1993

Death Date: December 12, 2015

Age at time of death: 22

Age he would be in 2018: 25

Children Left To Cherish His Memory: (Georgio Jr; Adrien Gray)

Your Memory Lives On Georgio

#SayMyName   #NeverForget

Chapter 4: You Too Can Help

Everyone tends to believe that once a victim dies and has been buried, the big part is over. They tend to believe they no longer have to be supportive or show any care or concern. The issue of gun violence however, is a universal one. Everyone must come together and tackle this issue head on.Take back our babies and let them know that we care.

◆Mothers, stand up and be mothers. If you don't know how to be one, ask questions. There is help out there.

◆And elders, stop judging. Use the wisdom you've gained throughout the generations to help uplift the next generation.

◆Fathers, step up and let your voices be heard. Our children need male role models back in their lives. You are a vital part of the structure within the home.

◆Neighbors, bring back a sense of community. Get to know your neighbors and their children. Know exactly who your children are playing with as well as who they are hanging with at all times. And neighbors, if you see your neighbor's child(ren) acting up or getting into trouble, please speak up! Let their parents know what you saw, what you did, and why you did it. It takes a village to successfully raise a child. ◆Grandmothers, PLEASE come back!!! We need those grandmothers that would get in your tail if you even thought about acting like you weren't raised right. It's okay to have age on you because length in years of life on Earth signifies wisdom!!!

◆Youth, learn to fight with your minds. You are powerful beyond measure. We need you to think before you act. If you unite and put your powerful minds together, you can overcome! With solid leadership behind you, you can change and make a difference.

◆The biggest thing that we all can do is build a spiritual connection. On top of that, PRAY...because prayer changes things.

<u>Be the Solution</u>

A statistic;

Another trouble ridden gang member;

A menace to society;

Another lost cause;

Is how some viewed me.

A robber;

A burglar;

Another troubled youth with a gun;

Is what some called me.

A brother;

A son;

A child looking for a way out of poverty,

Despair,

And hopelessness;

Is who I was.

Surrounded by crime,

Never hearing good news,

I accepted the only role known to get me a few quick dollars;

I can't say it was right,

But it was all I knew to do.

Although my actions were naïve and stupid,

My checkered past should not define me,

I was nothing more than a teen struggling to figure out life;

Unfortunately for me,

I was forced to do it,

In one of the worst housing projects,

Nashville, Tennessee has to offer.

A product of my environment,

Is what I became;

Leading the word criminal,

To be plastered in front of my name;

But that's their definition of who I was,

Because they never witnessed the stress put on my chest,

Just trying to survive,

While living in Edgehill Projects.

I can only leave advice in my untimely demise,

And it's directed towards both citizens and politicians;

Get involved!

Talk to the youth;

Show them something different;

Encourage them to keep pushing;

Let them know they have other options;

And when they mess up,

Don't just give up and forget about them.

Pick them up,

Dust them off,

Then set them back on the right track;

Perhaps I'd still be alive,

If someone had just tried.

No matter how many times they fall,

Stay on them,

And don't allow society to label them as a lost cause;

Fight for them,

See life through their eyes,

And you just might be surprised to find,

That a little love and tenderness,

Was all that was needed;

To reignite the spark,

In a troubled youth's eyes.

Dedicated to the loving memory of Lamar Hughes

Power in The Tongue

Your voice matters;

You can change a life;

All you must do,

Is stand up for what's right.

Sounds complicated,

Sounds like it comes with a lot of work,

But I beg to differ;

It's as simple as a compliment,

Or a hug,

A smile in the morning;

Or a small token of love.

A little help with their homework;

Or a football tossed back and forth a few times;

Or a listening ear;

Just show them some support.

Reward them when they do good;

Encourage them when they're down;

Motivate them to do right;

[109]

Instead of always beating them down when they do wrong.

You have the ability to change someone's mindset,

If you'll just open your mouths;

There's power in the tongue,

To take back our youth;

And have no doubt,

We can,

And we will take back our babies!

Dedicated to anyone wanting to make a difference in the lives

of our youth

<u>The Curse</u>

Violence has been the primary way of showing strength in the
streets;

And that's a stigma passed down over several generations;

A curse inherited at birth;

By every generation,

But it doesn't have to be.

It's past time for current generations to take a stance against
the growing epidemic of gun violence;

It's past time for us to fight for our future,

The doctors, leaders, teachers, lawyers, scientists, engineers,

entrepreneurs of the next generation;

It's beyond time to take back our youth,

And break this generational curse,

By any means necessary!

Reprogram their minds;

Show them being educated is cool;

Catch them while their young;

Expose them to a trade;

Equip them to work for themselves,

At a young age;

Help them to value the power of a dollar because they earned it

legitimately.

Lead and guide them down the right path;

Build them up,

When others seek to tear them down;

Restore a sense of pride deep inside their hearts;

Reveal the strength in their heritage;

Incorporate culture back into their lives;

Show them something different;

Teach them who they are.

Break this generational curse;

Make your presence felt;

Impact someone's life;

Don't let your existence be in vain;

Our youth can be saved!

It just takes a little persistence and dedication,

No different than any other goal one seeks to accomplish in life,

Don't give up on our babies;

They are our future after all.

Dedicated to those determined to make a difference in the lives of our youth

Chapter 5: The Void Left Behind

The void left behind once the trigger of a gun has been pulled is unexplainable. The pain, the hurt, and the sadness truly can't be put into words. However, sometimes the devastation caused by it needs to be seen for others to learn. Take heed to pain shared through the following interviews and really hear their heartache. It just might touch your heart.

#SayTheirNames

#NeverForget

#PutDownTheGuns

#JustLIVE

Loved One: Keith Battle

Person Being Interviewed: Rodgerick Waters

1) **How old were you when Keith died?**

   38

2) **Where were you when you received the news?**

   Home

3) **What is your relationship to Keith?**

   Best Fiend

4) **Has Keith's case been solved?**

   No

5) **If it has been solved, how many years was/ were the perpetrator(s) given?**

   Not Applicable

6) **If the case is not solved, has it at least gone to trial?**

   No

7) **Did Keith know his killer(s)?**

   Unknown

8) **What are your feelings toward the killer(s)?**

   "I don't care for them at all."

9) **Will you ever be able to forgive the killer(s)?**

   "Yes because of what I was taught in church but I will never forget what they did."

10) **If you were given the chance to ask Keith's killer(s) anything, what would it be?**

"Why did you do it?"

11) **How do you celebrate /remember the life of Keith?**

"I celebrate his birthday with a get together."

12) **What message would you give the youth concerning gun violence?**

"Put the guns down. It ain't worth it. Why are you doing it anyway? It's more in the school than it is in the streets. The streets ain't gone get you nowhere."

Loved One: John Sykes

Person Being Interviewed: Rodgerick Waters

1) **How old were you when John died?**

   38

2) **Where were you when you received the news?**

   My Godmother's House

3) **What is your relationship to John?**

   Brother

4) **Has John's case been solved?**

   No

5) **If it has been solved, how many years was/ were the perpetrator(s) given?**

   Not Applicable

6) **If the case is not solved, has it at least gone to trial?**

   No

7) **Did John know his killer(s)?**

   Most Likely

8) **What are your feelings toward the killer(s)?**

   "I have no remorse for them."

9) **Will you ever be able to forgive the killer(s)?**

   "Yes because of what I was taught in church but I will never forget what they did."

10) If you were given the chance to ask John's killer(s) anything, what would it be?

"Why did you do it?"

11) How do you celebrate /remember the life of John?

"I celebrate his birthday with a get together."

12) What message would you give the youth concerning gun violence?

"Put the guns down. It ain't worth it. Why are you doing it anyway? It's more in the school than it is in the streets. The streets ain't gone get you nowhere."

Loved One: Antonio Kelly

Person Being Interviewed: Antoinette Tibbs

1) **How old were you when Antonio died?**

   21 or 22

2) **Where were you when you received the news?**

   Home

3) **What is your relationship to Antonio?**

   Mother to his children

4) **Has Antonio's case been solved?**

   Not to my knowledge

5) **If it has been solved, how many years was/ were the perpetrator(s) given?**

   Not Applicable

6) **If the case is not solved, has it at least gone to trial?**

   Yes

7) **Did Antonio know his killer(s)?**

   Yes

8) **What are your feelings toward the killer(s)?**

   "Hard feelings. I don't hate him though."

9) **Will you ever be able to forgive the killer(s)?**

   Yes.

10) **If you were given the chance to ask Antonio's killer(s) anything, what would it be?**

"What made you decide to it now?"

11) **How do you celebrate /remember the life of Antonio?**

"I try not to celebrate it. I just look at my kids."

12) **What message would you give the youth concerning gun violence?**

"I really don't know."

Loved One: Lamar Hughes

Person Being Interviewed: Triona Bigsby

1) **How old were you when Lamar died?**

   20

2) **Where were you when you received the news?**

   The Grocery Store

3) **What is your relationship to Lamar?**

   Sister

4) **Has Lamar's case been solved?**

   No

5) **If it has been solved, how many years was/ were the perpetrator(s) given?**

   Not Applicable

6) **If the case is not solved, has it at least gone to trial?**

   No

7) **Did Lamar know his killer(s)?**

   No

8) **What are your feelings toward the killer(s)?**

   "Anger."

9) **Will you ever be able to forgive the killer(s)?**

   No.

10) **If you were given the chance to ask Lamar's killer(s) anything, what would it be?**

"Why would you kill him over a dice game when you could have been the grown man that you are and walked away?"

11) **How do you celebrate /remember the life of Lamar?**

"Birthday celebrations and visits to the graveyard."

12) **What message would you give the youth concerning gun violence?**

"Stop! Stop! Stop! Think before pulling the gun. Stop the killing."

Loved One: Georgio Gray

Person Being Interviewed: Rickia Moore

1) **How old were you when Georgio died?**

   20

2) **Where were you when you received the news?**

   At the Scene

3) **What is your relationship to Georgio?**

   Mother of his children

4) **Has Georgio's case been solved?**

   No

5) **If it has been solved, how many years was/ were the perpetrator(s) given?**

   "One got something like 20 years at 100% and yes I was satisfied with that outcome."

6) **If the case is not solved, has it at least gone to trial?**

   Currently in Trial

7) **Did Georgio know his killer(s)?**

   "Yes. They even hung out in my house."

8) **What are your feelings toward the killer(s)?**

   "Jail isn't enough. I wish his friends could have murdered them. I want their families to feel what my family does. It's not fair. I think of it daily. I still have nightmares. It's very hard."

9) **Will you ever be able to forgive the killer(s)?**

No.

10) **If you were given the chance to ask Georgio's killer(s) anything, what would it be?**

"Why? Why did you have to take it to that level and take away someone's dad?"

11) **How do you celebrate /remember the life of Georgio?**

"I carry his jokes with me. I have talks with his sister. I visit his gravesite on his birthday and sometimes I visit with his dad."

12) **What message would you give the youth concerning gun violence?**

"I really don't know. That's a question that I will have to think on."

13) **What would you like the world to remember about Georgio Gray?**

"No one can take his place. He matured me at the age of seventeen while teaching me how to be a woman. I will do anything to bring him back. His killers destroyed me and my children's lives.

Loved One: Jocques Clemmons

Person Being Interviewed: Sheila Clemmons

1) **How old were you when Jocques died?**

   "I had just turned 51."

2) **Where were you when you received the news?**

   At Work

3) **What is your relationship to Jocques?**

   Mom

4) **Has Jocques' case been solved?**

   No

5) **If it has been solved, how many years was/ were the perpetrator(s) given?**

   No Justice

6) **If the case is not solved, has it at least gone to trial?**

   "There was an investigation but no trial and no reprimand."

7) **Did Jocques know his killer(s)?**

   Yes; The Police

8) **What are your feelings toward the killer(s)?**

   "Angry, mad and upset in the beginning. I prayed and asked God to place forgiveness in my heart. I also sent word to the killer that he has been forgiven. If God can forgive, so can I. My focus on God has kept me centered. The weight was lifted when I spoke the words of forgiveness."

9) **Will you ever be able to forgive the killer(s)?**

"Yes. I already did."

10) **If you were given the chance to ask Jocques' killer(s) anything, what would it be?**

"Why didn't you taser him? Why wasn't one shot enough? Why didn't you let him go? You already had all the information you needed from the tags on the vehicle. What did you say to my son that day?"

11) **How do you celebrate /remember the life of Jocques?**

"I remember him as if he was still alive. I don't celebrate his death. I only celebrate his life."

12) **What message would you give the youth concerning gun violence?**

"Put down the guns because you're doing what they want you to do so they won't have to. If law enforcement asks you to stop, please just stop! When it comes to the police, I want to say that all police are not bad but some are. For police, find other alternatives to shooting. If you must shoot, shoot to wound instead of shooting to kill."

13) **What would you like the world to remember about Jocques Clemmons?**

"Jocques was a loving, caring person. He did so much good for so many people: family, friends, and community included. His heart was so big.

Loved One: Ronnie Foxx

Person Being Interviewed: Vickey Foxx

1) **How old were you when Ronnie died?**

   48

2) **Where were you when you received the news?**

   Home

3) **What is your relationship to Ronnie?**

   Mom

4) **Has Ronnie's case been solved?**

   No

5) **If it has been solved, how many years was/ were the perpetrator(s) given?**

   Not Applicable

6) **If the case is not solved, has it at least gone to trial?**

   May 21st begins the first trial.

7) **Did Ronnie know his killer(s)?**

   "Yes, they were friends. His killer was his child's mother's sister's boyfriend at the time."

8) **What are your feelings toward the killer(s)?**

   "I don't want him dead. I just want him to be punished I don't hate him."

9) **Will you ever be able to forgive the killer(s)?**

"No. Never."

10) **If you were given the chance to ask Ronnie's killer(s) anything, what would it be?**

"Why did you kill my son? I just want to know why."

11) **How do you celebrate /remember the life of Ronnie?**

"On his birthday, we barbecue and do a balloon release. On holidays, we do a balloon release. On his death anniversary, we do a gathering at McFerrin Center then we release balloons at the graveyard. This will be the last year for that however. We want to let him rest in peace."

12) **What message would you give the youth concerning gun violence?**

"Stop the violence. Stop the killing. Put the guns away."

13) **What would you like the world to remember about Ronnie Foxx?**

"Ronnie was a family person. He was a friendly guy. He loved basketball and he loved his son."

Loved One: Cheryl Phillips

Person Being Interviewed: Jacketa Bell

1) **How old were you when Cheryl died?**

   18

2) **Where were you when you received the news?**

   Across the street from her.

3) **What is your relationship to Cheryl?**

   Daughter

4) **Has Cheryl's case been solved?**

   "Sort of. We got two out of four killers."

5) **If it has been solved, how many years was/ were the perpetrator(s) given?**

   Not Applicable

6) **If the case is not solved, has it at least gone to trial?**

   "Trial begins in August."

7) **Did Cheryl know her killer(s)?**

   "One of them, yes."

8) **What are your feelings toward the killer(s)?**

   "I don't know. I don't give it much thought. I wish they could suffer the way I did. I don't have words when it comes to them."

9) **Will you ever be able to forgive the killer(s)?**

"As of right now, I'm not there yet. I'm not sure if I will ever get there."

10) **If you were given the chance to ask Cheryl's killer(s) anything, what would it be?**

"Who were they really after and why did they choose that particular time to go after them? Even if it was an accident, why didn't anyone come forward and say that?"

11) **How do you celebrate /remember the life of Cheryl?**

"I do what she would do if she was still here. I surround myself with family and make it a happy occasion."

12) **What message would you give the youth concerning gun violence?**

"Stop and think about the consequences. You're not just hurting who you're after, you're hurting everyone including yourself."

13) **What would you like the world to remember about Cheryl Phillips?**

"She didn't deserve what she went through. She was a very loving and caring person who would have probably tried to talk them out of doing what they were doing."

Loved One: Ronquez Bigsby

Person Being Interviewed: Lashelle Bigsby

1) **How old were you when Ronquez died?**

   29

2) **Where were you when you received the news?**

   Home

3) **What is your relationship to Ronquez?**

   Mother

4) **Has Ronquez's case been solved?**

   No

5) **If it has been solved, how many years was/ were the perpetrator(s) given?**

   Not Applicable

6) **If the case is not solved, has it at least gone to trial?**

   No

7) **Did Ronquez know his killer(s)?**

   Unknown but most likely

8) **What are your feelings toward the killer(s)?**

   "Right now, they're harsh because I don't know who the killer is."

9) **Will you ever be able to forgive the killer(s)?**

   "No. I don't think I can. They took my child away."

10) **If you were given the chance to ask Ronquez's killer(s) anything, what would it be?**

"Why?"

11) **How do you celebrate /remember the life of Ronquez?**

"I try to do gatherings with his siblings to remember him. I used to do candlelight vigils but I don't do those anymore."

12) **What message would you give the youth concerning gun violence?**

"That's not the life to live. Put the guns down. Don't throw your life away. You have your whole life ahead of you. Don't choose the cowardly way out. Your parents suffer because of your choices. Too many of our kids are being lost to the cemetery or jail due to gun violence."

13) **What would you like the world to remember about Ronquez Bigsby?**

"It's a lot that could be said. He was athletic, smart, kind, funny, and a very outgoing person. There was never a dull moment with him around. He was loved by many and loved many as well. He truly had a heart of gold."

Loved One: Antonio Kelly

Person Being Interviewed: Antwain Kelly

1) **How old were you when Antonio died?**

   18

2) **Where were you when you received the news?**

   At the scene

3) **What is your relationship to Antonio?**

   Brother

4) **Has Antonio's case been solved?**

   Yes

5) **If it has been solved, how many years was/ were the perpetrator(s) given?**

   "I'd rather not answer."

6) **If the case is not solved, has it at least gone to trial?**

   Yes

7) **Did Antonio know his killer(s)?**

   Yes

8) **What are your feelings toward the killer(s)?**

   "I dislike him but I'd rather not talk about it."

9) **Will you ever be able to forgive the killer(s)?**

   "I already have."

10) **If you were given the chance to ask Antonio's killer(s) anything, what would it be?**

"I don't know. No point in asking why because that's already known. I would ask if he hadn't died, would you have tried to shoot him again?"

11) **How do you celebrate /remember the life of Antonio?**

"I celebrate him daily. He's living through me.

Everything he told me to do before he died I'm doing it such as: sports, my music, and being the big brother to my family as he was to me."

12) **What message would you give the youth concerning gun violence?**

"Stay out of those type of situations and stay away from those kinds of people. Then you won't have anything to worry about. Stay focused on your goals."

13) **What would you like the world to remember about Antonio Kelly?**

"He was a great big brother, a great father, the best on the basketball court. He was the sorriest comedian. He was a pranking mentor who only wanted to see people do good."

Loved One: Antione Meeks

Person Being Interviewed: Shawonda Meeks

1) **How old were you when Antione died?**

   35

2) **Where were you when you received the news?**

   Home, asleep.

3) **What is your relationship to Antione?**

   Mother

4) **Has Antione's case been solved?**

   "In my eyes, no. There's a lot of conspiracies going around."

5) **If it has been solved, how many years was/ were the perpetrator(s) given?**

   Not Applicable

6) **If the case is not solved, has it at least gone to trial?**

   No

7) **Did Antione know his killer(s)?**

   "Yes. Some were considered family."

8) **What are your feelings toward the killer(s)?**

   "I have a lot of hatred in me. I don't do even for even. God is working on the situation and they're getting their karma."

9) **Will you ever be able to forgive the killer(s)?**

"I will forgive but I won't forget."

10) **If you were given the chance to ask Antione's killer(s) anything, what would it be?**

"I don't know. I would have a lot to ask after thinking on it. How can you take somebody's life and then lay down and go to sleep?"

11) **How do you celebrate /remember the life of Antione?**

"Graveyard visits but I struggle with them."

12) **What message would you give the youth concerning gun violence?**

"I wouldn't give the youth one. I would give their parents one. Know where your children are and what they are doing. Stay on these kids and get in their asses."

13) **What would you like the world to remember about Antione Meeks?**

"His smile. He was so much to so many people. He would give the shirt off his back."

Loved One: Jory Sweatt

Person Being Interviewed: Kendra Reeves

1) **How old were you when Jory died?**

   44

2) **Where were you when you received the news?**

   Home

3) **What is your relationship to Jory?**

   Mother

4) **Has Jory's case been solved?**

   No

5) **If it has been solved, how many years was/ were the perpetrator(s) given?**

   Not Applicable

6) **If the case is not solved, has it at least gone to trial?**

   "Trial starts in April."

7) **Did Jory know his killer(s)?**

   "Yes. They were classmates/associates."

8) **What are your feelings toward the killer(s)?**

   "I try not to wish death on him. I try not to hate him. I want to be the person that doesn't have hate in my heart but when I turn on the news, I want to see that he's been found dead."

9) **Will you ever be able to forgive the killer(s)?**

"I pray so."

10) **If you were given the chance to ask Jory's killer(s) anything, what would it be?**

"Why? Why my son? What did he do that was so bad that you felt like you had the right to take his life?"

11) **How do you celebrate /remember the life of Jory?**

"On his death anniversary, we've done balloon releases for the last two years. On his birthday, I have a dinner and invite family and friends but I'm leery of a lot of company because I never know how I will feel on that day."

12) **What message would you give the youth concerning gun violence?**

"Pulling the trigger does not make you tough. A two-year-old can pull a trigger. Anybody can pull the trigger of a gun."

13) **What would you like the world to remember about Jory Sweatt?**

"He was a good person with a big heart. He was a very caring person."

Loved One: Jory Sweatt

Person Being Interviewed: Shay Jackson

1) **How old were you when Jory died?**

   27

2) **Where were you when you received the news?**

   At his mom/my aunt's house.

3) **What is your relationship to Jory?**

   Cousin

4) **Has Jory's case been solved?**

   No

5) **If it has been solved, how many years was/ were the perpetrator(s) given?**

   Not Applicable

6) **If the case is not solved, has it at least gone to trial?**

   Trial starts in April.

7) **Did Jory know his killer(s)?**

   "Yes. They were classmates. We all hung out together."

8) **What are your feelings toward the killer(s)?**

   "I hope he dies a terrible death."

9) **Will you ever be able to forgive the killer(s)?**

"I've already forgiven him to heal and move on but that doesn't stop the fact that I hope he dies a terrible death. I believe in karma 100%."

10) **If you were given the chance to ask Jory's killer(s) anything, what would it be?**

"Why? What did he do to make you want to take his life? Why couldn't you just talk?"

11) **How do you celebrate /remember the life of Jory?**

"On his death anniversary, we've done balloon releases for the last two years. On his birthday, we have a dinner with family and friends."

12) **What message would you give the youth concerning gun violence?**

"There are other alternatives to what you have going on such as sports, instruments, painting, art, etc. to let out your frustrations. Anything is a better alternative than picking up a gun."

13) **What would you like the world to remember about Jory Sweatt?**

"He was a great person. I believe he was angel sent here to help those he helped."

Loved One: Jocques Clemmons

Person Being Interviewed: Todd Bryant

1) **How old were you when Jocques died?**

   31

2) **Where were you when you received the news?**

   Home

3) **What is your relationship to Jocques?**

   Best Fiend

4) **Has Jocques' case been solved?**

   No

5) **If it has been solved, how many years was/ were the perpetrator(s) given?**

   Not Applicable

6) **If the case is not solved, has it at least gone to trial?**

   "There was an investigation but there no trial or justice."

7) **Did Jocques know his killer(s)?**

   Unknown but it was the police.

8) **What are your feelings toward the killer(s)?**

   "I'm numb towards the situation."

9) **Will you ever be able to forgive the killer(s)?**

   "I already have."

10) **If you were given the chance to ask Jocques' killer(s) anything, what would it be?**

"Why?"

11) **How do you celebrate /remember the life of Jocques?**

"By having his sons around me. They remind me so much of him."

12) **What message would you give the youth concerning gun violence?**

"Guns are not good. They are the wrong way to go."

13) **What would you like the world to remember about Jocques Clemmons?**

"He was a great man, a great father, a great leader, a great friend."

<u>Words of Appreciation</u>

◆*Special thanks goes out to everyone who has played any part in the making of this book and the stance it takes against gun violence. I appreciate each of you, your understanding and your willingness to be a part of what the Hood Love volumes represent.*

◆*Special thanks goes out to each and every person that has purchased any part of the Hood Love volumes (be it electronic or paperback) and received the messages told through the unfortunate and untimely deaths of the victims involved. I personally want to thank you for listening to the pain shared in their stories.*

<u>Play Your Part</u>

Now I must ask something of you…

◆I humbly ask of you not to allow the deaths of these victims,' their stories or their lives to be in vain.

◆I humbly ask you to help spread the messages found in this book and the volumes before it as well as the future volumes to come.

◆Share this book with anyone that you encounter.

◆Do your part to help save our babies please.

Remember the face that forced life into this movement...

My Nephew, Ronquez A. Bigsby

Follow the Hood Love

Volumes...

Hood Love: Ain't No Loyalty In It

Hood Love 2: The Streets Still Ain't Loyal

Hood Love 3: Take Heed To The Warnings

Available at:

R4Presents.tictail.com

Amazon.com

Booksamillion.com

Also,

Hood Love 4: Warning Before

Destruction will be released

October 16, 2018!

Made in the USA
Columbia, SC
26 April 2024

34651335R00085